There's a Ghost in this Machine of Air

There's a Ghost in this Machine of Air

Poems by Iris Jamahl Dunkle

WordTech Editions

Published by WordTech Editions
P.O. Box 541106
Cincinnati, OH 45254-1106

ISBN: 9781625491619

Poetry Editor: Kevin Walzer
Business Editor: Lori Jareo

Visit us on the web at www.wordtechweb.com

Acknowledgments

Thanks to the following journals and publications for previously publishing the following poems:

"Find Lake Ballard" and "The 100 Year Flood, 1986" *Poecology*, Issue 5, 2015

"Sweetbitter" *Cider House Review* 2014 Volume 16, Issue 4.

"Geography as Seen from the Tall Ships" *Cider House Review* Volume 15, Issue 3.

"Weight of Abundance" "The Accidental Pull" "After the 1915 Apple Show" "The 66th Apple Blossom Parade, 2012" *JMWW* Spring 2013

"A Language is a Map of our Failures" *Midwest Review* 2014

"Tending the Sedge" *Catamaran* February 2015

"Pleasant Hill Cemetery, Sebastopol, CA" and "Moon Over Laguna de Santa Rosa" *Digging our Poetic Roots Anthology*, 2015

"Home is an Uncanny Valley" and "Hybrid Algorithm" *Talking Writing* 2015

"I Have Envy Enough" *Sugarmule* volume 47, 2015

"The Llano de Santa Rosa Rancho, 1843," *Kudzu House* 5.2 2015

"Prelude" *pacificREVIEW* 2015

"It Was Not an Emotion I Knew By Heart," "When I Die Bury Me Where the Fog Rests," "Life Gathers Around the Fire" *Tinderbox* 2015

Thanks to the many friends who read and gave feedback on these poems along the way. A special thanks to Tayve Neese who helped edit the final manuscript and to Dorinda Wegener who designed the cover.

Additional thanks to The Laguna Foundation and Gaye LaBaron for their knowledge of our wetlands and local history and to the Bodega Heritage Gallery for allowing me to use this historic "Oak and Stream" by Grace Myrtle Allison Griffith (the daughter of Nathanial Griffith who was considered the father of the Gravenstein Apple). Grace (along with her two sisters) appear in the poem, "The Accidental Pull".

Most importantly, thank you to my husband Matt, my sons Jackson and Maxwell and my parents John and Rebecca Johnson for their continued support.

Table of Contents

Ghost Fruit: Gravenstein

Laguna de Santa Rosa

Sweet Odysseus: Early Settler

Hybrid Fruit: Winterstein

"I walked
New Year's Day

beside the trees
my father now gone planted

evenly following
the road

Each
        spoke"

—Lorine Niedecker

"What Americans mean by history is anything they think they can forget."

—James Baldwin

Ghost Fruit: Gravenstein

Dear Sebastopol –

Hard not to get dizzy, here, under tides of scent—
how they grade and terrace the air:

> salt thick tang of wet earth fat with limestone
> against sweet rot of wind falls.

Pine sap town built on stolen ground.
Wagon rutted streets. Hills once lush

> with redwood and oak, cleared
> to the root for acres of orchards.

Century-wide berths of scrub oaks
smoldering in the Laguna de Santa Rosa.

> A train that carried its screaming
> weight down Main Street for nearly 100 years.

But the WPA mural on the post office wall
still frames the hard won promise:

> neat rows of apple trees
> flanked by white chicken coops.

Once, your accepted story swallowed me under its bell glass sky.

> Now, I wake slowly. Learn to waver
> in the air above what history we've learned,

sense what's pushing up underneath.

A Language is a Map of our Failures

At first, the land was covered in thick redwoods; their dizzying tops spindled the wool of low fog. They lived in open meadows between trees. Close enough to the sea to dream of salt and the muscular bodies of fish.

The smoke that rose from the *kotchas* was thick with oil, but the scents still wove together: fog's breath, rosemary, the burning of wood.

The oldest ship appeared out of the fog like a hollow, wooden whale on the blue horizon. Then, two smaller wooden boats skated toward shore. No fear drifted on the slack winds, even though this was the day when change would begin to rise, ash-like, into the air, catching and burning in the branches of the tall trees.

The map would show memory's retreat as it bled further and further inland: rocky sand to cliff to the high meadows where the trees had begun to fall. There would be many more ships. There would be much forgetting, until the towns came: a small dry-goods store, then a livery, and a blacksmith. It was after all this that the history was recorded and it was without what had been lost to air, to the eaves of trees.

Geography as Seen from the Tall Ships

From lull of dank, wet wood and passage, too many bodies
pressed together; our clothes bleached and worn thin
from sun's glare and winds incessant blowing.
From the sway that had pooled and gathered in us
like a brackish bilge until we were unable
to understand land, that line of shore defining an end,
then from it the green hills pouring back into
what we were meant to discover. From the weak legs
that strode from the small boat into icy
surf came uncertainty and doubt. The weight
of cargo carried across then dragged off
the ship and over the grassy dunes
to the waiting wagons. There were no maps.
There were only ideas and a strange man standing by
the wagons. Still wet, we gathered again
close, but far away from what we knew of
ourselves in the rough wood cabs. Two rutted
tracks leading a dusty path out from months
of salt and sway, over the roll of hills.

Sweetbitter

1

In the 1700s Prince Carl of Denmark eats Gravenstein apples while visiting the dappled shade of an orchard in Italy. Its rigid trunk offered the cuttings of an idea that would take to graft at his summer home: a white castle on the blue lip of the Baltic Sea. Seeds planted, then tended until great orchards bloomed across the flat low lands where the sea seeps in slowly, where salt, like history lingers on the air. *Tart-sweetness bulging from a red-barred orb.*

2

By the time the orchards grew into vast bounding fields, the Germanic spoken legends of the North Sea were receding like the tide as were the resources. Entire islands of stories were swallowed whole in a storm.

3

For a century, gardeners cut and grafted the bone-barred heart of the fruit to perfection: until it tasted bittersweet enough, until it kept long enough to travel large distances. Then, the seeds and cutting were slipped into the trunks of steamship passengers. Tiny seedlings kept moist across long passages. Until the Gravenstein seedling was carefully unwrapped from its moist, burlap coverings to be planted here in Sebastopol on freshly clear-cut hills that rolled to the sea.

4

In the 1850s, those who didn't find gold farmed. Orchards covered the bare hills as fast as they were cleared of scrub oak and pine and Miwok. And the years seeped in. The horticulturalists grafting to win a longer market, a higher yield. But, what the apple bore was memory: a long traveled, bitter-sweet taste that can't be bred out or baked out or forgotten.

Red lines that bind the fruit to the hands that pick to the stories that still whisper on the low roll of a long traveled sea where salt, like history, lingers on the air.

There's a Ghost in this Machine of Air

Salvation can be found before light comes when the dawn chorus tightens the fogged air. Then, sun rises to reveal the massive green hills rolling back to the sea. The Irish immigrant who first tried to settle Kota'ti built a rough planed cabin on Crane Creek, and planted wheat. After a season passed, he was surprised in the middle of night by the ones whose land he had stolen: dozens of young Coast Miwok men running bare-chested down the sloped flanks of the fog wet hills, their arms extended into fiery wings; their hands clutching the three feet of burning Tule that hissed and popped from their arms. Can't you see them now? Fiery birds ghosting this machine of air. The settler would escape but his cabin and wheat fields would be burned to the ground. He would never return to the rolling green hills, to the dawn chorus, that had hypnotized him because after that night he understood why one might run, arms aflame, to save this.

Planting Gold Ridge Mid-1800s
for the Roberts family

On steamships crossing cold depths:
horizon slurs away— blue blur of what is left behind,

to seas of tall grass, tides of wind. Bumped and roughed
across dull plains, over snow covered mountains.

Days jostled between wagon slats until we reach the edge
where the sea tries desperately to reclaim the land.

Then, walking up hills damp with redwoods fronds
into valleys of wide-armed oaks, until we find a clearable plot.

Weeks digging out the wild to the root: felling redwood and oak,
grubing out the stumps and roots to avoid oak root fungus.

Then, walking behind a donkey pulling a plow slow
through cleared fields until hope forms.

Knee deep in that new dirt—in the scent and stain of it—
fingers mound and plant careful rows of fragile seedlings.

For weeks pacing the rows watching the tiny trees worry
with rain, sway and bend nearly flat when wind rips from the sea.

Then, the widening of the trunks, the waiting on the wide porch
for things to grow and open as the stars sharpen and come into view.

Hint of pink buds like perfect tongues.
Then, hillside igniting into confetti of delicate pink blossoms.

The globes forming until burden weighs,
branches propped with braces.

Walking the rows like a child unable to wait.
The up at dawn readying bins and ladders.

The long days of twist of wrist to drop fruit.
The sticky arms and sweet smell.
The bins filled with fruit.

Susurration

Tule sway in the wind carrying song
from creek bed to creek bed: Atascadero Creek

born on English Hill where the sea lingers on horizon
like a forgotten idea, flows back over

Gold Ridge to town then veers away toward
Green Valley. And all along that blue song

moans, fog and limestone, above, then below
the ground. From patchwork hills where orchard leaves

murmur reverently back until there is a song spoken
in pale pink blossoms that rise from

each trees' green budded, but dark, delicate fingers.

I Must Go Out and Find Something Else to Hate

Besides the pink-petal blossoms that flag
the untrimmed trees that continually line
the passage of potholed roads carrying
me away from their embrace and this place.

I must find something that is more deadly
than arsenic and lead to kill what spreads
uncontrollably: mistletoe, cankers
mildew, flies, and my need to always look back.

I must watch the hills roll out toward
somewhere else where the fog rests. I must
site a single tree rising on the hill's
sloped, broad back, and know it as a sign.

Even as the wagon slows, even as
the dust rises to blind us of hope.

I Have Envy Enough

I have envy enough for the net of
swallows that skim and dive through golden air.
For the place their fragile bodies protect:
the white shuttered house already shadowed,
the water tower, the two lonesome palms.

Envy enough for the ridge of tall pines
that seem to hold the wide blue sky aloft
by pointing their crooked wills toward ascent
for the hawks' nests they carry year to year
for that searing cry, for the dark lean

of shadows over the house, over the steep
graveled drive that follows the creek out.

Gateway

When there were just the two worn ox-cart ruts:
a road traveled between the lumbering
camps in the Russian River Valley and
the mouth of the Petaluma River
that which was needed was built roadside:
a few saloons, a blacksmith shop, a general store.

The few who stopped were welcomed by the scent
of the tall pines that crowned the hills above
and the wide prairie of the Laguna
where oaks rose offering a majestic, dappled shade
that reflected in the lakes. What the town would become,
months, years later was still written in the minds
of those passing through. Body stiff from
too many hours sitting at the helm
of the massive cart, the mind wanders, spins
cities out of fields, spells fortune out of stars.

The Washoe House

House made of dawn, house made of thunderous hearts;
bricked in; gone cement silent; mouths full of dust;
walls still whirring, still breathing like hummingbird wings.

Downstairs, you can still see the roadhouse and bar built in 1859;
a dusty stop on the stagecoach route between, Petaluma and Santa Rosa.
Built on *Roblar de la Miseria,* the house still straddles Washoe Creek.

But rise up the stairs past the rose flowered wallpaper,
dollars flagging the ceiling like so many tongues
and the house quiets. Closes in on you like deep water.

As if, the women who once pleasured passing men
for a small pinch of gold dust were waiting
on the other side of the walls. Their breath fogging the glass
between truth and what we chose to tell.

The Naming of Sebastopol in Mudtime

Frontier towns are built
of new lumber: still sticky
with sap, still fat with water.
What you build in the past
retracts—shows cracks—places
where the wind can lick clean.
Sebastopol is a town that dreams
its name again and again.

The story goes: two men,
Stevens and Hibbs, stood face to face
on the main road in a town called Pine Grove.
Anger erupted. Fist to fist.
They were up to their knees in mud.
The naming is what happened after:

Hibbs running away into Dougherty's General Store.
Stevens following but stopped at the door:
You ain't coming in! Instead, Stevens paced
the muddy street outside the store as Hibbs hid inside.

For hours his feet rutted the deep mud with his story.
Until, passersby stopped and watched,
until someone recalled the year long siege
of Sevastopol during the Crimean War, and the name stuck.

From this incident, the town took its name,
said early historian Robert Thompson.
A source filled with cracks, no way
to check one hundred year old facts.

At that time of Sebastopol's naming,
there were six other towns named Sebastopol.

Was each born of a standoff? There is only
the strength of a story built out of time, mud and pine,
set solid enough in the ground to keep so many seasons later.

When I die, if I go to a place where there are apples, I'll know it won't be heaven

After the tractor cooled and dust settled
come into house gone cold. Stoke fire's coals.
Peel and slice the windfalls thin, brown sugar,
a lemon plucked yesterday from the bough.
Roll dough cold. Cover. Bake an hour. Gather
the children. Coax. Read words or written. Stir
pot hot on iron stove. Wash the earth from
crooked carrots and beets. Slice thin into
caste-iron skillet. Stir and fry with yesterday's
slaughtered chicken. Wash the young faces.
Scold the ones who know better. Divvy chores: set,
serve eat, clear, wash, scour, hot steam boiled.
Lay the children down. Look for quiet enough.
Sit beside the glowing coals, song pouring
back into the fire what's burned out.

Every Hour is Saved

Each day a new field plowed and planted.
Each season production would swell.

Each fruit handpicked into wooden crates,
delivered by wagon then truck to the packinghouse.

Then, the small, red-striped globes
were carefully placed into shipping crates.

The tiring stand of ten hours a day
sorting the good from bad. Women's work.

Close-doored, but checkered with sunlight
brought in through the high windows.

It was a dull, quiet work that could
open or close the wilderness of mind.

Decades later, when their bodies had grown old,
and their minds strobbed memories——that wilderness

(however conquered) would return in a few lines
by Tennyson about an old king who traveled

far and couldn't return home: *but every hour is saved.*
How those words illuminate the musty smell

of the packing house, the ache of feet,
the practiced ballet of young hands,

and the hum of low voices staving off silence
by repeating the few poems they'd known by heart.

After the 1915 Gravenstein Apple Show

"The Gravenstein Apple has, above all others, proved to be the money winner in Sonoma County. It is a healthy vigorous tree. It always bears a good crop, never over-bearing, as many varieties do; is of the best quality of all known apples"
–Luther Burbank

After the logging, after the plowing,
the planting, the yield, most hills stood slightly
bereft but ever producing apples.
To celebrate the escalation of
apple sales, the Sebastopol Apple
Growers' Union raised a tent across from
the train depot, began the Gravenstein
Apple Show in 1910. Photos show
uniformed boys lined in neat rows, women
dressed in white floor-length dresses, entering
the sawdust-floored tent. Inside, the warm air
swelled with the scent of tart, picked apples
architectured into sculptures that set into form
a history of the apple, the town. Fictions or truths
built out of the bittersweet fruit yielded
gristmills, locomotives, a gold ridge farm,
even *Gold*, a Petaluma river
steamship that shipped the apples down the slough
to San Francisco Bay. Until war closed
the fair and that same steamship was loaded
instead with the cargo of men and boys,
their arms still browned from the season's harvest,
their eyes looking back to the golden hills.

Before the Union Man Caused the Apple Strike

Oily sun leaks through the clouds
as I crouch in the dark
warming my hands by the small fire
I've coaxed out of the dead branches;
coffee pot still mute and breathless.
Around me lay the bodies of those
not long lost to sleep; those who shuffle
in canvas bags, trying to keep warm.
In an hour we'll be kicking up dust
at the Hoyt's place, clearing one tree
after another. Until noon when we break
under the shade of those trees, eat our supper
and close our eyes. It's a different sky
one sees lying on turned earth
looking through the leafy branches
toward whatever the clouds spell.
Until the bell sounds
and you get up and are at it again
for another row. By the time
we return to camp, we are too tired
to play cards or drink. Instead,
we sink back into that same earth
looking up at a sky gone mute
with dark, listening to the prayer-like
mumblings of the nearby creek.

The Accidental Pull

Nathaniel Griffith brought Luther Burbank to his orchard
on the flat marshland of the Laguna. From his home the trees
spelled across the wide expanse in straight rows.
Already, they were good servants—yielding
a ton of fruit each. But the season was
short. Burbank had ideas for winter fruits:
the Winterstein, still bittersweet tasting,
but with tougher skin to withstand the frosts.

The three girls could see the men on the porch
as they sat in the skirt of soft grass surrounding
the willow. Spring had covered the grass
between rows of apple trees in yellow
mustard. They made a game of following
the strokes of color—the low freckle of mustard,
the high powdery acacia, to the solitary exclamations of
yellow iris crowning the front yard. Years
later, after Burbank's experimental
trees had failed, after their father had died
and the green wooden farmhouse had burned down,

they would remember this inventory:
how that day the golden lines had burned in
them a tether to this land. And each day
after they would try to pull themselves back.

There Lies the Thing I Most Desire

for the Furusho family

Dark oaks spun their crippled fingers over
the star-slurred sky the night our family left
our apple orchard for internment camp.
Now, we live in horse stalls where air is stiff
and void of fog. I've paced these wooden planks
worrying futilely over the harvest
we left behind day and night but there is
no wind here strong enough to carry my
prayers back to our temple Enmanji.
Now its name, garden of fulfillment, stings
like a slap in the face. Letters from the Holte
and Williams boys promise to pick and sell our fruit
but trust is difficult to plow here—
from each stall whispers root and spread like rot.
There is no way to dig it out like the oaks
we cleared from our field before we planted.
There is only the stiff wind,
the press of powdery stars into our longest night.

The Mother Tree at the Luther Burbank Experimental Farm

In the late 1800s, Luther Burbank declared
Sonoma County "nature's chosen spot"
and sold the rights to the first
Idaho potato to fund his journey out.

At his Experimental Farm,
he solved problems—how to grow
cactus without thorns; how to grow
apples year round. He checked
the pockets of every visitor
for fear one of his prized seeds
might be carried away
on something other than wind.

These days, there are less visitors.
But, Shasta daisies still greet
those who come with big toothy grins.
Toward the back, near Pleasant Hill Cemetery,
the Mother Tree looms large and full,
always bearing fruit, always bearing
another graft or possibility.

Under brace, her branches
are so full, they seem
threatened even in a light rain.
Arms extending over the fence,
as if guarding what is left,
as if beckoning the ghosts
back from the earth,
back from the fog as it burns off.

Luther Burbank Garden, Santa Rosa

History seems bricked in——but the soil
remains rich between the cracks, where the big-
toothed grins of Shasta daisies can spring forth.
If something doesn't suit you than graft it
to something else. Sometimes, a potato
seedpod small as a fingernail can sprout
ten futures thick with eyes; the largest sold
for passage on a train to another
life where the fields pulsed. Where onion skin-thin
paper journals were used to trace the shape
of each creation's potential, weighing
risk against what could bloom against all odds.
When you leave, you must empty your pockets.
Let the wind unwind the lost paths to home.

Freestone

Hope is a town quarried from easily
worked sandstone. First, a general store
built on button candy and dry goods.
Then, the black-velvet air of the saloon
that gathers the work men like a hive.

When the architect built the two-story
hotel those men began to leave their canvas tents
and settle down. This is before the train
drew a silver line between product and deliveries
made possible by the Sausalito Ferry.

Years before when the frog chorus
still swelled from Salmon Creek,
General Vallejo gave the land
to three men who were named James.
So, together, they built a sawmill on

the creek's stony jaw. Soon, they became
three men gone drunk on the wealth of land
and what more they could dredge out of it,
became red-faced, chest to chest,
spit, and hot sparks shaving the dark

until one man (call him James)
decided to saw the mill in two
revealing what was underneath:
frogs song on top of sweet water on top
of a rich bedrock that would build the town.

Laguna de Santa Rosa

Moon over Laguna de Santa Rosa

A rueful moon drifts over Laguna de Santa Rosa tonight—
river that flows both ways carrying history heavy on its back.

Those who first recorded what they saw were in awe
of the wooded plain, ripe with water and animal life.

But change was quick and drastic. First, the cattle ranchers
cleared and burned the Valley Oaks leaving their blackened bodies

to girdle the golden Tule fields. Then, the Gold Rush
increased the price of game—white and gray geese, ducks,

deer, antelope, elk, even the few grizzlies that had survived
were caught and sold on the docks of the Petaluma river.

The remaining oaks were split and corded, or reduced to charcoal.
Then, channels were dug to drain the cattle farms.
Then, the sewage ponds dug and filled.

Today, the moon hangs low in the sky.
Not full, just a thin crescent illuminating a single path back,
past the remaining oaks, past forgetting.

Prelude

Begin by walking the cracked, chamomile-paths.
Let the path stretch across a wide stubbed field.
Fill the air with the sounds of birds.
Fill the air with fat bees and the machine hum of insects.
Post appropriate markers that mark miles but not the whole truth.

Try to contain the fissures of time in each quick step.
When you walk under the lone oak that constellates the field
like the last visible star, smell smoke.
See the ghosts of hundreds of other thick oak trunks
that once crowded this space.
Hear their lost leaves whispering.

When you reach the man-made lake
constructed to replace the natural lake,
walk the perimeter. Observe the cattails
that cage the floating bodies of seven pelicans
that have stopped here to rest on route back to the sea.

Look out across the drought-dry field
and imagine a chain of hundreds of lakes
linking their way back to the sea.
Drain them for the good soil underneath.
Fill them with soot.
Fill them again with feces and urine.
Cover what's left of them in brambles.
Get tangled in the sticky blood of berry juice.

And when you near the last of the water,
the floating pontoon bridge,
and the sounds of children playing baseball
in the dirt on the chalked diamond,
let a red-snake T-bone the trail.

Let it open in you a wound that, at its center, is a mouth.

Tending the Sedge

The land was first the lands. Then, the Pomo,
the Miwok and the Wappo lived on it.
The triblets of the Konohomtara,
the Kataictemi and the Biakomtara
settled on different sections of the wide
Laguna for over 10,000 years.
Little changed except the roots and stalks of
the course sedge plants that grew half-submerged in
the water. The Pomo basket weavers
cultivated the sedge fields, passed prayers
for straight stalks and supple roots from mouth to
ear to mouth. Prayed and sang, untangled and threaded.
The basket is in the roots, that's where it begins.

The Llano de Santa Rosa Rancho, 1843

Jose Ramon Carrillo was granted three leagues of forested delta or llano
thanks to his brother-in-law, General Vallejo. Soon, acres of oak forests
that seemed to breathe light into dark were cleared. Laikes drained.
Crops replaced sedge with corn, wheat and barley. Trees were burned for charcoal.

But even as the trees thinned, the plain still teemed with large game:
great herds of muscular elk forged the remaining lakes,
mountain lions paced their territories and rested
in the eaves of oak and ash, and grizzly bears
roamed the wet land at will. Then, there was the day
when Jose was out riding across the eastern edge of his rancho,
and one such bear followed him.

His horse, wild with fear, stumbled into one of the many sink holes
that had opened up in the changed land, fell ten, maybe twenty feet
followed by the leaping, growling bear.
It was in that dark mouth that the three tangled into a story.
From which first, a bear would emerge,
somehow lifted from that dark hole and released unharmed;
from which the man and his horse would follow, equally unharmed.

What commerce was exchanged to obtain this outcome
is dark and dangerous as that opened pit.

Leaving only the question:
How will we emerge from the story we have fallen into?

Lake Jonive

The largest of the lakes were made into
resorts. There are photographs of young
women with parasols, sitting erect
in boats afloat on the large lakes; wooden
docks where bodies hang and thread arms against
a weightless dark. All was for the taking.
Until 1895, there was great
bounty and no limits. Any man could
pull a hundred fish from the Laguna's
chain of lakes. San Francisco was hungry
for fresh game. A bushel of mallard ducks
brought a gold nugget. For those who stayed to
farm, lakes on their land became land reclaimed:
drained for the rich soil that waited underneath.

The Lesson of Mud and Potatoes

"History comes in many forms — some of it, apparently, edible."
–Gaye LeBaron

What a citizen wants is to peel back
the skin of history that shields a place:
the single story that survives record.
Time offers its own flood—washes out roads
of thought no matter how deep the ruts run.

To ask what it was like to be a passenger
on Bill Tibbetts' bone-jarring stage coach
riding from the docks of the Petaluma River
to the potato mines of Bodega
where nutty-flavored, red-skinned potatoes
thrived in the salty, mineral soil
until blight wiped out the crop; until we

forgot to tend the road between then and
now. When landmarks like Spud Point
loom mysterious instead of marking
the story they once told: a barge too full
of potatoes that sunk on the spot.

How to still imagine each stop the stage
took in 1860 after winter rains
left roads nearly impassable
mud to our knees, wheels stuck in ruts
but the Laguna gone swollen and fertile,
offering us passage across
in the steam engine ship Georgina.

What questions should a citizen ask to dredge this out?
So we can dig up a few forgotten tubers of those lost potatoes,
so that we can find that tin-rusted hull of a ship,
to carry us back to a place that speaks in more than one voice,
which we continually rewrite and remember.

Marine Mammals of the Northwestern Coast of North America, 1874

The whaling captain Charles Scammon left
the ragged, rocky cliffs of Maine's coast for
San Francisco in 1849 where he led many whaling expeditions.
But what those large bodies gave instead of flesh and oil
was a path to a luminous blue, Baja Lagoon
where the whales stilled their bodies to give birth.
The first day he arrived at the open-mouthed bay
his heart shifted into a locked wooden chest
left rib open and bare. He learned to observe
for different purpose: not to hunt, but to know
what the dark bodies could spell into him.
When he left that unpredictable sea to write
it all down he settled with his son on the edge
of the Laguna where the sea still spoke in susurrations of fog.

Finding Lake Ballard

What they said was *we ruined the water*
not we rewrote the land with dynamite
and the pulsing, yellow jaws of backhoes.

When they said rev up your mind, what they asked
was for you to contain a lake—call it
Gray's or Ballard. Let it spill forth

over half a mile. Let it straddle
a hundred yards of earth. Cover its banks
with exclamations of ash and willow.

Dig it deep enough that catfish and bass
linger in the shadows. Then, let doubt
fill you like a balloon. Go belly up.

Try to recall the blue bloom of sky seen
from this angle: dark, cold water pressing,
no, holding you up; warm sun on your face.

To know is to dive deep into the sediment
of what is no longer possible to find.

Wait at the closest train station: Mount Olivet
for someone who has a memory made from
spun clouds whose footsteps can stitch

back the lost route of Mark West Creek
whose sediment was used to fill in the lake,
the acres of low spots on the ranch.

When they ask you who ruined this place
answer with a tongue made of peach peels

and a mouth full of sewage. Your eyes backlit
with dynamite and the smooth shine of dirt.

Laguna as Sebastopol's Sewer, Beginning in 1906

As the town grew, so did the waste. Buildings,
still sticky with pine sap, were built in a day.

Hope packed incoming train cars from San Francisco.
Soon, Sebastopol became known not only for its soil
and plentiful game but also for its smell.

Raw sewage filled street culverts, and dripped from
gutters, until sickness descended.

City Officials were pressured to find a quick solution
and so giant cesspools were dug out and filled
with all of the waste Sebastopol had to offer:

urine, feces, apple skins and cores,
animal remnants from the tannery,
peach skins and pits, rusted cans and broken bottles,
even the giant skeletons of cars.

All piled up. Formed a dam between
what was waste and what was not—

time circling the Laguna
in the body of a white egret
waiting for a chance to land.

The 100 Year Flood, 1986

"But people are like that about natural disasters. Everyone believes that the history on any place began the day they arrived." —Gaye LeBaron

Memory is as uncertain as islands
that rise in a flood—you don't know what lurks
underneath. A silver boat can split this
seam of water: even gone muddy, gone
untold for so long. Disasters rise and stay
like high water marks in the unconscious
and each day after is checked against it.
What do we have to fear? The worst already
happened, couldn't happen again.

But the river, like a muscular animal,
overtakes the banks, chews up asphalt, rises
more to fill stores and homes. Until
the whole Russian River Valley is filled
with her muddy, pulsing body
regardless of what history you remember.

Escaping the Flood, Child's Eye

The children awoke to the adult voiced shout of *wake up*.
By this time, it had rained continuously for three days.
The night before, the newscaster's thick mustache
had barely risen as he warned:
floodplain, 100-year flood, prepare for the worst at high tide.

When they rose from bed and walked to the window
they could see the backyard had been transformed.
The chicken coop roof was an island
in the grip of a fast flowing river.
Then, the adult lead the children down the wet, muddy-floored hall
toward the gaping frown of the front door where water
licked hungrily at the front step. Just over the threshold
a small silver boat stuttered on the frothing brown water.

Fossil

Crossed sticks catch
silk of soot—keep
sink down from *rise up*.

The Laguna has an eye made
of passing clouds over glass heart.
Made of crossed sticks that catch

the wax and wane of time and shores.
Some have reclaimed.
Kept *sink down* from *rise up*.

Some have dug under for pay dirt;
blown open blue skies with dynamite.
But even crossed sticks can't catch time.

No one to protest, but the birds
herons who cartoonishly wing the air—
keeping *sink down* from *rise up*.

Or, the bright bald shine of earth:
metal-jaw scraped into submission.
Crossed sticks can't catch shores.

Somewhere in each lake resides a story—
whether real or forgotten.
Whether is rises or sinks.

Stories that flap uselessly in the wind.
Or, that spread their oily sheen
over the sticks that mar the surface.

What if a story sunk heavy enough

into soot, into tang of limestone,
that it became some lost animal body,
bones crossed like sticks,
whose memory could still rise up to meet us?

Impaired

Which system is miraculous?   The plentiful before or the rescue of what's left after?

This 14-mile wetland, this 254-square mile watershed that's spread between four cities where history's left over sediments are still being removed. By 1990, 92% of the Laguna's riparian forest was gone.

Left arm reaching into Copeland, Washoe and Blucher Creeks. Right arm reaching into Santa Rosa, Hinebaugh and Five Creeks. A mouth that breathes into Mark West Springs Creek.

A backbone made of the Mayacamas and Sonoma Mountains.
In summer months, the Laguna becomes a silver ribbon of water that threads.

In winter she loses boundaries becoming again the series of lakes that lead to the sea.

Listed as impaired under the Federal Clean Water Act for sediment, nitrogen, temperature, phosphorus, mercury and dissolved oxygen.

When you walk the smooth, grated paths or the dirt paths that line the fields, or the tree-dappled paths remember the miraculous ghost of what was once there.

Sweet Odysseus: Early Settler

This is the House of Yearning

This is the house of yearning where fog-combed skies mute the cries of red-tail hawk.

This is the day when the wind carried salt, lavender and rosemary.

This is the day when it was dull enough that memory lit the mind like a tiny lantern.

A long journey in an open wagon. Clouds of dust. Swarms of flies. The ever turning reel of clouds overhead and the slow stories they'd unwind over days that stretched wide as a sea.

The hard boards on our backs lying down in the wagon. The ruts in the road as seen through the cracks and every once in a while the bright shock of a wildflower.

The smell of fire and smoke. The sound of fire licking the found logs, popping on wet spots. The press of bodies around the fire. The way the fire quieted, then glowed like a red, sunken star.

How each day we'd speak of the house. How we'd build it with shared words. You'd say: hillside, open. I'd say: water whispering, dappled woods.

How always there was an orchard and a garden.

And the miles wound under us. Flat swaying seas of grasses becoming the rise of thick-knuckled mountains. How the air tightened, grew crisp.

By the day we sat at the blue-eyed lake, we'd constructed everything out of air.

As we bathed in the icy water. As we washed the dust and flies and miles from our bodies we were submerged in the shadows of birds.

Today the house is made of wood. The orchard stretches twenty trees deep. The garden writes itself into the soil.

And you, my sweet Odysseus, are not in it.

Under Warning of Birds

The fog lingers in the corners of things: crotch of hill, the edge of blue sky left smudged.

Yesterday, under the oaks and pines, blue jays erupted into a cloud of sound and warning.

When I looked up to the spinning trees, every one rustled with their weight and sound.

We had gone to the creek to find solace from the heat, from the work of the day, but we found only warning.

I could feel time coil itself like a snake. That's when I gave him my memory.

The place is like that, I say. It's a place to linger and forget. He laughs. Already able-bodied as his buried Pa.

A simple S-shaped bend in the creek. Limestone-bedded. The gentle trickle of a summer waterfall nosing the leaning ferns.

If we listen to the birds, if we watch the sky, if we follow the press of guilt and duty, we'll never see what is hidden in the dark water.

It only takes a few found sticks. A willingness to find the hidden life of salamanders and crawdads to clear the creek of what keeps the water from flowing.

Dead leaves, silt, a tree branch, stones.

In a few weeks, the harvest will begin. Already the tart green orbs burn from the fingers of trees.

When we plowed the field, dust veiled our life. Even this morning I was still sweeping dust from the wooden floor in front of the stove.

Even under warning of birds, joy enters our bodies at the corners unbidden and smudged.

A Hircine Hillside

The day we found it, the hillside was stone laden, dense with tall pines, thick oaks and scrub brush.

There were no man-made paths. Only the careful thin trails of deer wandering like cursive in and out of brush.

The man in town say's we've got to dig all the oaks out, even the roots. Or they'll cause our apple trees to rot. He said.

So, on the first day, we sat on a limestone outcropping feeling the weight of it all: the bodies of the tremendous oaks we'd need to fell and split. The scrub we need to clear.

For a week we dug until our backs tightened and ached. At night we'd sit side by side by the small fire pressed down by the powdery stars.

He thought of the goats first. *Why not?* He asked.

The next journey into town we loaded the wagon with flour, salt, sugar and two full-grown goats. I'd traded my mother's coral cameo for the lot.

Each day we'd tether the goats to a new patch of shrub and they'd eat it clean as a washed slate. Each night the stars would loosen their powdery stare.

The bodies of oaks fell with a loud crack. You could feel the weight of them carried from the soil to your knees to your heart.

It's the wood of those trees we used to build the house. Each one carefully sanded down.

Some days looking out of the house toward the hillside now covered in apple trees I still see that wilderness pressing back in. Some days when the fog is low I still hear his voice as if it is trapped in the bowl of this valley.

But the words I begin to use to answer back are made of air. Are left lingering, like wisps of fog, in the tops of redwoods.

How to be Enigmatic

The young red tailed hawks must be learning to fly. Their piercing cries reverberate across the valley loud and without cause, as if they have just found their voices.

But their small feathered bodies take to the velvet summer air effortlessly, and we watch their bodies glide as if on ribbons.

How many seasons have we watched the hawks rear their young in the tall pine, teach them to fly the line from pine to pine above our home? How many seasons before we found this place had the birds been here?

Then, there are the red faced foxes that dart, low to the ground across the field at dawn and dusk. Some days they carry a catch in their mouths. Some days they return home empty.

And the coyotes who howl in packs at night.

We still carry ourselves as if we are borrowing this place.

Even that first season when we labored for five days with the hired Allen boys laying the foundation for our home: long, swollen days of hard work and desperate thirst.

Then, with the boards set, we lay on our backs on the hard wood bathing in the light of a full moon, listening to the unseen residents around us move and settle into night.

How we realized then what we now know, that what we see and hear are tiny glimpses of what lies hidden underneath.

We cry and cry like the young hawks to an audience of air trying to find our home, our center, when all we need to do is glide.

Cañada de Jonive

Some days I wake to a world blanketed by fog. A single sound –
hammer striking rock, or hawk's cry, reverberates in the bowl of
valley until it sounds intimately close.

It's these days when I know I need to find a path out. Hitch the
wagon. Gather Joe and head down the rutted hill toward a town.

We live between two settlements.

Over one hill lies the sandstone quarry town, Freestone and farther
on Bodega and Bodega Bay where the dark blue sea breaths.

Over the other hill lies Sebastopol and beyond the expanse of the
Laguna de Santa Rosa.

Today, I choose the closet route: drive up the steep hill toward
Freestone where there is a railroad station and a general store.

We can check the post office for any letters from back East. We can
eat lunch at the hotel and watch the weight of the metal railway
engine pull away.

As the wagon rolls slowly through rutted redwood groves the sounds
around us sharpen. Our horse whinnies. The summer creek babbles.

And Joe's voice startles me. Mama, he whispers. Yes? I say, eyes still
stretched ahead, hand's steadied on reins. Why are we alone?

In a place like this I don't believe in lying to a child, even a five year
old.

We aren't alone. We are stitched together me and you. I say, cracking
a smile. But it's just me and you because Papa is gone.

He pulls his small body closer to mine on the buckboard, so close that I can feel the hummingbird whir of his heart.

The day we found our homestead was the first day we entered this town. It used to be called the Cañada de Jonive. This was before the railroad. It was a rough settlement.

It was a place where if things couldn't be solved they were cut in half with a lumber saw.

The man at the hotel had told us about Dawson and McIntosh. How Dawson had cut their shared house exactly in two with a saw because McIntosh hadn't included Dawson on the deed.

The deer leapt out of the bushes suddenly, spooking the horses. Joe cringed into me. My heart leapt into my throat. The wagon bed rocked, nearly tilting on the steep slope.

And then I saw it blink. Our life, however run down it had become, stared me in the face like a wild animal and I loved it even if I couldn't tame it or catch it.

The deer passed back into the dark trees. Our horse snorted and steadied. The wagon creaked back into place and Joe and I held each tight and breathed.

How Do You Teach Pain?

Look deep into the delicate shafts of dark railway tunnels and forget the light.

Remember the press of dirt.

The way air burns away.

Gather blue stars of forget-me-nots, constellations of Queen Anne's Lace, the sweet smell of wild pink roses.

Listen to a wooden house ache in winds that sweep up at night.

Follow footprints before they are swept away.

It Was Not an Emotion I Knew By Heart

For weeks, we had picked and stacked and boxed the fruit.

The thick sweet smell of ripe fruit followed me everywhere.

Yellow jackets swarmed the fallen fruit.

Days swelled thick and bloated until they blurred one into the next.

Then, the lightening came.

The way the wagon's wood base rose without the weight it had carried once the apples were sold.

The way my body unwound over miles, and finally settled.

The way sleep spilled deliciously over the dark night like a dark, overpowering joy.

When I Die, Bury Me Where the Fog Rests

I can't remember where I was when he last spoke. Time was stained-glass shards glistening in the light, but fragments drift in memory like a low fog:

When I die I want my body buried here where we've worked so hard to build our place.

Were these words spoken over a campfire as we traveled west under press of stars?

Or, did he breathe them through swollen lips as his body lost its strands of life?

If I go first, bury me close to you and Joe.

And so we did. You can see the wind-washed fence that surrounds his grave from the stairs landing. Each wooden picket is covered in lichen. But I can still smell the turned earth of that day each time I step to it and kneel.

When I die bury me where the fog rests.

How I wished to follow his body into the grave. How only Joe's tiny body clinging to mine kept me from letting go.

This is a hard life. Marry again. Don't be alone.

Had he known when he spoke these words how impossible they would be? Seasons soar past. The bare trees burst into blossoms, green out and then fruit. The plentiful harvest. Then, bare again and again.

When I die I want my body buried here where we've worked so hard to build our place.

I still walk each row wearing his old work boots, my arms sinewy with sun and work. My heart gone stained glass, but mended. The way an apple graft takes - one branch grows into the other, carries on.

On the Days I Was Consistently Wrong

The first few weeks after my husband's death the Allen brothers would come by every other day.

Their tall willowy bodies tethered me to the earth and to the task of watering and plowing the rows.

On the days they weren't there, I tried to walk in their shadows, tried to match footstep for footstep, task for task. But, I was always consistently wrong.

The coffee would burn. Joe would howl. The dust would take to the air in clouds.

And each tree looked impossible to trim back. I couldn't see the lines that the Allen boys seemed so effortlessly to find.

Pretend you are looking at the stars, I'd hear him whisper.
Remember how you could never see the forms when we first started off?

And I'd repeat to myself under my breath: *Virgo, Pleiades, Cassiopeia.*

I would try to remember how the powdery stars became the shapes he described, as I walked each leafy row.

Until my body learned the motions of the ranch. Until the shapes emerged from the trees.

For Purposes of Spirit Lifting We Visited the Sea

Joe and I rest on the rocky sand in bare feet. He is restless. He jumps up and runs as far down the shore as his tiny body will carry him. I let him run.

I'm too tired to move and he is too filled with joy. In a few moments I see him, a tiny speck, racing the sandpipers as they run back and forth with each lace of wave.

A flock of heavy bodied pelicans soar over us.
The day is clear. So clear that for the first time in months, everything seems possible.

My fingers find the debris that's washed up around me: blue flat stones, smooth driftwood, and a single piece of abalone shell that seems to gather sun.

Sitting on the flat beach I see the rock lungs open and close with breath.

The cold blue expanse of sea rolls out with all that is carried under it, all the way to the blur of horizon.

Life Gathers Around the Fire

The breeze that gathers today whispers in the bay and oak leaves of the forest that surrounds the orchard.

I am walking the rows. Looking at the way the bulbs swell on the tips of each branch. Small, tart orbs ribbed with red stripes.

Harvest looms ahead: the sweat and then relief of it.

Tonight the fog doesn't come in and Joe and I sit outside off the porch tending an open fire and watching the stars slowly emerge.

We gather around the fire and tell all that has happened in the day.

The Allen boys with their news of town. Who crashed their buggy on the racetrack. What opera is playing in the opera house. Who has fallen sick or died.

Then, Joe leans back placing his strong arms behind his head and says. *Tell me a story, Ma.*

It is the same story each time. Another chapter out of the Odyssey. Only, we don't stick to the plot. In our version, Odysseus never did find his way home but continued journeying on.

Island to island.

And so it is each night and so it has been since he was just a boy. I dream up another island out of air and we step upon it and inhabit it under the starry night.

A Message to Myself
So I Remember Who I Am
Wagnon Road, 1898

Removed from the troubles of everyday life—the mind opens like a sky stirred by sea wind.

Memories blow in, thin and pale, then bloom up into cinematic stained sails.

What message does each carry?

These days they only cloud.

I imagine the jagged crown of dark trees on the far ridge can hold them back.

As if mercy were fair.

But it's likely only tiredness that inks my mind clear of the hope's fireflies.

Some days, like a phantom limb I can still feel to itch, I can feel his soft lips on mine, his strong arm around my waist.

And the pile of days that have been gathering since his death are heaved off, thin clouds that they are, and driven back to sea.

After You Left, I Let the Woods Speak for You

We landed here swollen in belly and mind; threw our backs into it—
cleared the land until it was tamed into rows.

But, the perimeters, those dark woods, push in, gathering back what
we've claimed.

Some nights, when the moon pools through bubbled glass, thin walls
seem to fall away to let in a chorus of coyotes.

Their song feels close and permanent. As if all that we've hatched
down and sorted into rows will be dug up and reclaimed by morning.

As if my loneliness has finally found a voice——a duet to sing against
the moon's haunting silver pool.

You should have never taken the work.

There was enough.

On that last day, driving the oxen up the steep climb toward
Freestone where the tunnel would collapse and take your life, you
turned back and waved.

Your hand white, like a flag, an offering toward what would pursue
us for so many stitched together days.

What We Wish the Stars Not to Tell

I never want to be too comfortable with what we've done.

Even, when Gravenstein apples hang heavy on the thin trunked trees.
When the rows are plowed to dirt.

Even when the wind dies down and lets the dust settle.

I never want to see what's lifted us out of our past.

Joe is not a child anymore. He's tall and strong, arms thickened and
browned.

Some days, when I let myself stop and breathe, and see your ghost in
him:
your wide forehead, your blue eyes, your cathedral smile.

To him you are less than a memory—some sweet Odysseus I conjure
up at night.

I can still remember holding Joe's plump toddler hand as we lay on
the porch to see the stars at night:

that one there is where we began out East; that powdery path is our journey west
where we found you, the brightest star at our center.

These days our loneliness has grown sturdier like the trees. It
stretches out in long, neat rows—

and if we ache enough, bend, break enough, your ghost flickers past.

Hybrid Fruit: Winterstein

Hybrid Algorithm

at Luther Burbank Gardens, Santa Rosa

Sensory garden, medicinal garden, garden of starts and failures.

To question history is to watch the chaos of its particles
glisten into discernible patterns.

We loosen embedded stones with our toes
among the trees that grow into each other.

We ask: *where is he buried?*
Light caught in the fingers of trees.

We ask: *where are the unattested species recorded?*
Indecipherable writing in notebooks
sketches of leaves, a seed as big as a child's fist.

Please do not record inside
Please do not disturb the war of air outside.

What's pushing up—ache of earth against this litany—
from mind to mind to mouth to air

patterns illuminate— a rustle of leaves
from the ghost of a fallen tree –Cedar of Lebanon.

The breeding between what will be,
and what will be left for us to believe.

Split

Most winters thanks to the teeth of rain, hills
glow green. Apple trees scarecrow up from rows.
Throbbing in winter light toward spring's reveal.
One never knows how many orbs will rise
and grow from the reach of stagnant branches.

In 1942, Twin Hills Ranch was seeded on 40 acres
by the Hurst family. Soon, it grew to become hundreds.
Each winter, an army of green budded trees covered
the hill next to the cemetery and the school, revving into production.

In the afternoons, children walked over to buy an apple or
a handful of candy. Parents would pick up bags of apples,
or loaves of apple bread as the kids played on home-made swings
cut from old tractor tires, or dizzied themselves
spinning on an old wagon wheel.

Some days the air would fill with the sound of children's voices.
Others, it would grow heavy with ash.

When time walks in the door, he's got muddy
boots. He leaves footprints you can't scrub out.
Even now, as the ranch stands gated, tin roof slouched,
the few remaining trees offering bare branches to the sky.

Pleasant Hill Cemetery, Sebastopol, CA

Old gravestones like granite-tongued love poems
cover the dead, forgotten farmers who now rest
in the soil they once plowed and planted.

Their arthritic trees that fence the grounds
in straight dirt rows are surprisingly still
fruit bearing after decades of neglect.

School children who walk past the orchards grab
the delicate branches and shake. The dead
have lost their need to feed their bodies, their

children's bodies. So, no one scolds them for
wrecking the fruit. The air pulses with
the pink confetti of apple blossoms

and joy rains down onto graves.

Pay Heed

Shadows of clouds passing over hills
reveal a barn bleached and de-boned by time
now without use except as makeshift shelter
for a few cows who linger during rain showers.

There was once a Gravenstein apple tree
that bore more fruit than any other. Here,
on this lip of ridge. In the photograph,
the giant tree fans out, fattened with fruit,

in a screen of leaves big as a house
behind the Arnold family: Minnie,
John, E.W., Meta and Vivian.

What future looms from the sky:
clouds passage blooming dark
into the tree's massive shadow
passes over their faces like history,
like an unknown oncoming storm.

We are writing these things
so that our joy might be complete

Unfettered joy is hard to tether down:
sunlight sifts through fans of redwood branches
rolling hillsides blazing in pink blossoms
tang of bay, smell of deep forest wet earth,
surprise of what rises from what is left.

Joy that carries on wind can rise again
and again. Joy stitches words in passing
clouds.   Even in the leaden hour, dark spot
growing on the horizon, to become
history. Joy spreads itself thin as sea
to cover everything in the salt of truth.

Prayers for Trees

At night the light rain percusses prayers onto
the tin roof of our barn; prayers not meant
for our sleeping minds or motionless forms.
They are prayers for those last scattering
of pink apple blossoms strewn carelessly across fields
as the gnarled trees stand steady against wind
in the wide green field. Prayers for those trees
as they thicken with green leaves, and gather
the promise of tart, ripe fruit. By morning,
the storm will be gone, the trees near bare of blossoms,
and we will wake without knowing about
the prayers whispered in the dark of night.

The 66th Apple Blossom Parade, 2012

The whole town seems over-exposed in bright
new sunlight on the day of the Apple
Blossom Parade. We stand four-thick watching
our children in uniformed marching bands
pass by, the shined up fire trucks throwing
handfuls of bright candy, and the old men,
who continually ride their old tractors
or apple sprayers down the parade route.
Showers of cold water arc out of old machines
that once carried lead and arsenic to
keep an orchard clean of unwanted pests
and the hot parade watchers beg for it.
All along the parade route the woman appears.
She spreads her golden wings and dances
next to the marching band. Then,
appears again in front of the fire truck.
We laugh at her. Shoo her off. Think her
a fool. But she returns, dancing and smiling.
When the parade stops, we gather children
and the streets are swept. We go home to fallow
fields still freckled with unpruned trees, still warm
from sunburns, still thinking of what's passed us
by as the fog rolls in and sedates us.

Sonoma County

At eye level, the field is pilose,
dew-weighted grass
rich with the scent of wet earth.
The soil here hums, electric—
since 1920, Sonoma County
has been in the top ten
for agricultural production.
There was so much open
land on which to plant crops
of hops, grapes, prunes and apples.

Already the apple trees
stand their hills clad in green gowns
and vineyards hold back the earth
in the maze of their branches.
At night, the air is fresh and alive
with all that desire—

a fox screams her needs
night after night
as we wish for sleep to bring us back
to the time before
when life throbbed, thrived.

Home is an Uncanny Valley

If the rain continues
then we may lose our escape down the gravel-throated drive.

We are hungry for the rain.

If the rain edits the earth of the fields,
if the rain rewrites the soapstone creek bed,
if the ditches we dug into the earth just yesterday overflow,

then the path back to ourselves could be blurred by the many
rainstorms before: 1987, 1992, 2005;
each flood, spilling into the next like a series of connected lakes.

The child looking out the rain freckled window could be ourselves.
We are hungry for the rain. We are hungry for the truth.

The reservoirs are low exposing what we'd forgotten: old logs, rusted
cars, a body or two.

If we flood again
then we could forget the hunger,
then we could forget what's underneath, exposed.

If home is an uncanny valley and we walk toward it,
see that it is too much like ourselves to believe

then the fields, the creek beds, the gravel throated drive
will scream muddy loud.

The child looking out the rain freckled window could be ourselves.
We are hungry for the rain. We are hungry for the truth.

Let home = null/washed new/a place built upon a place.

Let memory fade like a fog.
Let the child at the window be my child, not myself.
Let the water find its path back.
Let the rain spell out a truth on the tin roof above our sleeping heads.

Let path out open like a mouth.

Weight of Abundance

On days when sun blazes hills awake,
when still damp earth aches dark possibilities,
when crooked teeth of dilapidated barns
and crumbling stucco of lost missions
hum with stories they cannot forget,
I look at my freckled hands and try to find
a cartography for this desire to know
that seems stitched into me, into any
who live where one wakes to a horizon
that is continually blurred by low fog.

Stories are as abundant as the trees
and vines that are repeatedly heavy
with fruit. *What to dig up? What is enough?*
In a garden so thick with weeds, sustenance
bleeds with what is pressing upon it. So
days slur past, fat and happy, until
the eye sights it driving past, or the hoe
upturns the hidden artifact.

The Linguist Staff

is covered in ears. Not real ears, but carved,
extruding, so each grip reminds fingers
that the ears exist. There is no need to pour these
ears onto a table to illustrate a point.
Instead, through touch, the linguist speaks
from the ears. When he holds the golden staff
and speaks, he knows the ears are listening.

Perhaps this is a way to proceed on the rutted path of history.
If we keep our fingers locked tightly on those golden ears
perhaps we won't forget that the past is listening,

that the past expects us to circle back
and look under what we think we know
even if the path has become so overgrown

that we are lost.

Iris Jamahl Dunkle's debut poetry collection, *Gold Passage,* won the Trio Award and was published by Trio House Press in 2013. Her chapbooks *Inheritance* and *The Flying Trolley* were published by Finishing Line Press in 2010 and 2013. Her poetry, essays and creative non-fiction have been published widely. She is currently co-writing a new biography on Jack London's wife, Charmian London. Dunkle teaches writing and literature at Napa Valley College. She received her B.A. from the George Washington University, her M.F.A. in Poetry from New York University, and her Ph.D. in American Literature from Case Western Reserve University. She is on the staff of the Napa Valley Writers conference and co-facilitates the book discussion group at Jack London State Historic Park. Visit irisjamahldunkle.com for recent publications and upcoming readings.

CPSIA information can be obtained
at www.ICGtesting.com
Printed in the USA
FFOW02n1313091215
19486FF

9 781625 491619